# Given Up On Purpose

## How God Uses Rejection, Abandonment, and Pain to Reveal Destiny

**Aljenon Cooper**

# COPYRIGHT PAGE



ISBN: 979-8-218-92601-4 (Paperback).
ISBN: 979-8-234-00434-5 (Hardback)
ISBN: 979-8-234-01684-3 (eBook)

First Edition
Printed in the United States of America

# DEDICATION

This book is dedicated to the woman who chose love when she didn't have to — the woman who prayed for me, raised me, believed in me, and covered me.

To my mother, who showed me that being given up does not mean being unloved.

And to every person who has ever been rejected, abandoned, overlooked, or misunderstood — this is proof that your life still has purpose.

# Table of Contents

# FOREWORD

**By Pastor John F. Hannah**

There are some books you read, and then there are some books you feel. This is one of

those books.

Given Up On Purpose is not just the story of one man's journey — it is the story of so many

who have silently carried wounds that never had language. It is for the child who waited at

the door for someone who never came. For the adult still trying to make sense of why they were overlooked, mishandled, misunderstood, or left behind. It is for the gifted ones who

serve faithfully while bleeding privately. It is for those who learned early what it meant to

live with unanswered questions and unhealed places.

Aljenon writes with a transparency that is both refreshing and courageous. He holds

nothing back. With raw honesty, he takes us through the rooms of his past, the corners of

his heart, and the sacred moments where God met him, healed him, and revealed purpose inside every painful place.

What I appreciate most is this:

He does not present pain as something to be ashamed of — he presents it as

something God uses.

And he proves it.

Through Scripture, he shows us Joseph, Moses, Peter, David, and even Jesus — all who

walked pathways that felt like rejection but were really divine direction. Through his

testimony, he shows us that God does not simply redeem our story ... He rewrites it. He uses abandonment to align us. He uses brokenness to build us. He uses what we survived

to shape who we are becoming.

Many people assume that being given up is the end of a story. This book declares it is often

the beginning of one.

To every reader holding this book — you are holding evidence that God wastes nothing. Not

the tears. Not the trauma. Not the questions. Not the confusion. Every chapter of your life

has been intentional. You were not overlooked, you were hidden. You were not rejected, you were redirected. You were not given up on — you were given up for purpose.

Aljenon Cooper is living proof.

And after reading this book, I believe you will be too.

Love ya,— **Pastor John F. Hannah**

# AUTHOR'S NOTE

This book was not written from theory; it was written from tears, prayers, questions, and ultimately, revelation. For a long time, I wrestled with the reality of being given up at birth. I carried questions that many people carry, but few know how to voice...You were not given up by accident. You were given up on purpose. — Aljenon Cooper

# Introduction: The Purpose of Being Given Up

Her words echoed in my spirit that night:

"It is your purpose in life to discover your purpose in life."

In that moment, I began to wrestle with a deep and honest question: Does my life really have a purpose?

What is purpose, you may ask? Purpose is the reason something exists, was created, and something was done. But many of us—especially those who've walked through pain—struggle to believe we were made for a reason. When you've faced the hard parts of life—childhood trauma, abuse, abandonment, rejection, addiction, divorce, or just sheer disappointment—you can start to believe your life is some random accident rather than part of a divine plan.

This book is your wake-up call: your life isn't random; it's intentional. No matter how your story began or the challenges you've faced, your life carries an undeniable purpose. Maybe you were given up at birth. Perhaps you were born from a one-night stand. Maybe your mother doesn't even remember who your father was. Possibly you were told you were a mistake, an accident, or simply "not part of the plan." Maybe your family history is full of poverty, brokenness, or dysfunction. Maybe you're battling a disability, dealing with abandonment, or struggling to understand your worth.

But hear me clearly: God has you here for a reason.

You are not a mistake. You are a miracle in motion.

The Bible says in Jeremiah 1:5 (NLT):

"I knew you before I formed you in your mother's womb. Before you were born, I set you apart . . ."

Before anyone could label you, leave you, or limit you—God had a plan for your life. Yes, God's plan is good—but let me be honest: it doesn't always feel good. Sometimes life takes you in what seems like the complete opposite direction of your purpose. That detour is called the process. The process is not punishment—it's preparation.

And preparation never feels easy. It's uncomfortable. It's lonely. It's painful. It will test everything in you. But it is necessary. Purpose without process is potential left unrealized. Before the promise, there's always a process. And yes, the process may look like betrayal, abandonment, isolation, or obscurity—but it's all part of the divine setup.

God isn't as committed to our comfort as He is to our character. And sometimes, what looks like rejection is really redirection.

The Bible is full of stories that echo this truth.

- Joseph was given up by his brothers, thrown in a pit, sold into slavery, and imprisoned—but God used it all to position him for the palace. What looked like a series of tragedies was actually training for his destiny.

- Moses was given up at birth—placed in a basket and hidden in the Nile. But he was found by Pharaoh's daughter and raised in the royal court. God used his journey—from the water to the wilderness—to prepare him to lead His people out of bondage.

- Peter was impulsive, unstable, and unqualified in many people's eyes. Yet Jesus looked at him and saw more. He said, "I've prayed for you that your faith won't fail." Peter's denial didn't disqualify him—it developed him. He would become a foundational figure in the early Church. And then there's me.

A lot of people see me today and assume I've always had it together—that maybe I come from a long line of ministers or spiritual leaders. But that couldn't be further from the truth. I was given up at birth by my biological mother because drugs had overtaken her life. My very beginning was marked by rejection. But God had a plan. He placed me in the arms of a praying woman who raised me with love, discipline, and the Word. Still, I had to wrestle—internally—with what it meant to be given up. I struggled with identity, belonging, and feelings of abandonment. But now,

I see that what felt like rejection was really God's redirection.

Being given up wasn't the end—it was a divine setup.

This book is not just my story—it's a declaration for the child who felt the cold absence of a parent at every school event, the sibling who watched their brothers and sisters be chosen while they were left behind, or the individual who spent years trying to prove their worth to a world that seemed to overlook them. You're not disqualified. You're not disowned by destiny. You've been given up on purpose—for a purpose.

You may not understand every chapter of your life right now. As one philosopher said, "Life is lived in forward but understood in reverse." But I challenge you to keep turning the pages. Stop focusing on the pain and start focusing on the purpose. Trust that God is working all things together for your good—even the broken parts.

So, welcome to the journey. This is not just a book.

It's a reminder, a revelation, and a roadmap to discovering that sometimes . . . the very thing that tried to break you was the thing God used to build you.

# Section I — The Foundation: Purpose in Pain

# Chapter 1: The Betrayal That Led to Destiny

Joseph has to be one of my favorite biblical characters. I admire so much about him—his boldness, his resilience, and, most of all, his unwavering belief in the dream God gave him. Joseph is proof that God has many ways to get us to the place He's destined for us. His story reminds us that sometimes betrayal isn't a barrier—it's a bridge. Joseph's story begins with a dream.

He came from what many would consider a dysfunctional family. His father, Jacob, favored him, but his brothers hated him. The same Joseph who was wrapped in his father's love was also surrounded by jealousy and rejection. It's an interesting dynamic—loved and hated at the same time. Maybe you can relate.

Joseph had a dream that one day he and his brothers were in the field binding sheaves, and his sheaf rose above theirs, while theirs bowed down to his. He shared the dream, and his brothers didn't take it kindly. Many people criticize Joseph for speaking up, saying he should've kept his dream to himself. But I disagree. I believe that sometimes your destiny can't be activated until you open your mouth.

Some things don't begin to move until you declare them.

Joseph spoke—and the hatred intensified.

"Do you really think you will reign over us?" they asked.

But what inspires me about Joseph is this: he kept dreaming. Even after being met with mockery, rejection, and envy, he dared to dream again. This time, he dreamed bigger—the sun, the moon, and eleven stars bowed to him. The second dream drew even more opposition. His brothers "hated him yet the more," and his father rebuked him. But take note—the bible says his father observed the saying. Deep down, Jacob sensed there was something divine in what Joseph had shared.

This is a word for someone: don't dim your light just to make others feel comfortable. Don't downplay your calling, your gifts, or your dreams to make insecure people feel adequate. Be unapologetically bold. Live out loud. Dream bigger. Because one way or another, God's purpose will prevail.

Let's not forget the coat of many colors. Before Joseph ever dreamed, he was marked by favor. His father gave him that coat, and though Joseph wasn't the oldest, God chose him. This coat wasn't just fashion—it was prophecy. It was a sign of priesthood, of leadership, of divine calling. And that's something we must remember: God has the power to break protocol to position His chosen. He'll bypass tradition and reverse the order, putting the coat on the one He called. But that coat stirred something in the hearts of his brothers. One day, Jacob sent Joseph to check on them while they were in the field. Now, if you ask me, that was a rookie move. When you know someone is hated, you don't send them unprotected into enemy territory. But maybe that's the point—some of the pain we've endured happened because we were entrusted into the hands of people who didn't have our best interests at heart.

His brothers saw him coming and plotted to kill him.

They thought eliminating Joseph would eliminate the dream. But someone should have told them: you can't kill what God has purposed to live.

Reuben stepped in and convinced them not to shed his blood, planning to rescue him later. So instead of killing him, they threw him into a pit. And here's where many of us can relate. We know what it feels like to be left in the pit of rejection . . . the pit of abandonment . . . the pit of betrayal . . . the pit of being overlooked. But here's the truth:

Every pit has a purpose.

And while Joseph sat in the pit with no food, no water, and no help, his brothers sat nearby eating bread—as if nothing had happened. These weren't friends who pretended to be related. These were blood brothers. How cold-hearted do you have to be to feast while your brother suffers?

But while they were eating, a caravan of Ishmaelite merchants came passing by on their way to Egypt. And one of the brothers had a new idea: "Let's sell him." For a few silver coins, they exchanged their brother's life for profit.

This is why we must be careful around people who love money more than they love people. The Bible says, "The love of money is the root of all evil"—not money itself, but the love of it. When you love money, you'll compromise character, betray blood, and sacrifice anyone for the next check.

And so, they sold Joseph. But what they didn't realize was this: God was in the plan. Psalm 37:23 reminds us, "The steps of a good man are ordered by the Lord." Even when those steps lead through betrayal and bondage.

To sell Joseph, they first had to pull him up from the pit. Let that sink in—the same ones who threw him down had to lift him up. God will use the very people who tried to bury you to bring you out. He'll make your haters your elevators. He'll use the hands that tried to hurt you to push you toward your destiny. But here's the question for you to ponder: What is your pit? What situation or setback have you been thrown into? Take a moment to reflect. Because while the pit might seem like the end, it could be the very place God starts to elevate you.

Joseph was given up by his brothers.

And maybe you, like Joseph, have been given up on by the people closest to you. Maybe you were just looking for support. Maybe all you wanted was to be seen, to be loved, to be believed in. But instead, you were betrayed. Lied on. Abandoned.

But hear this: God still has a plan!

Joseph would endure more—slavery, false accusation, imprisonment—but every chapter was leading to destiny.

He was not being buried—he was being planted.

Joseph is sold into slavery—and now, he finds himself in Egypt, working in the house of a man named Potiphar. But here's what amazes me: even in slavery, God's favor follows him. Joseph may have been stripped of his coat, but he was never stripped of his calling. Potiphar quickly recognizes Joseph's excellence, integrity, and the divine favor on his life. Joseph is promoted and entrusted with everything in Potiphar's house. Scripture tells us that Potiphar left everything in

Joseph's care—he didn't even concern himself with what he had, because Joseph managed it all.

And then . . . here comes the test.

Mrs. Potiphar, seeing that Joseph was well-built and handsome, began to desire him. She tries to lure him into an affair. She wanted Joseph to sacrifice his purpose for a few moments of pleasure.

But Joseph refused.

He understood something we must all come to grips with: purpose is greater than pleasure. It wasn't just about saying no to sin—it was about saying yes to destiny. Mrs. Potiphar became more aggressive. One day, she grabbed his coat and tried to force him, but Joseph ran. He did what many people today struggle to do—he fled youthful lust. He left his coat behind but kept his character. And still, he was falsely accused. Mrs. Potiphar framed him and claimed he tried to violate her, and Joseph was thrown into prison for a crime he did not commit.

He was given up again.

But even in prison, the favor of God stayed with him. And that's something I need you to know—when God is for you, it doesn't matter who is against you. Favor can follow you into the fire. Purpose can still live in the pit.

In prison, Joseph meets two men—the chief butler and the chief baker, both from Pharaoh's palace. They each have a dream, but neither understands what it means. Joseph, still walking in his gift despite being in prison, interprets both dreams correctly. He asks just one thing: "When things go well for you, remember me."

But time goes on—and they forget.

Until one day, Pharaoh himself has a dream that no one can interpret. That's when Joseph is remembered. Pharaoh sends for him, and Joseph interprets the dream perfectly. The interpretation—and the wisdom with which he delivered it—was so profound that Pharaoh made Joseph second in command over all of Egypt.

The slave became the governor.

The prisoner became the prince.

The one who was given up became the one everyone had to go to.

Years pass, and a famine hits the land. Everyone—including Joseph's own brothers— must come to Egypt for food. Joseph is in charge of the distribution, and on the day his brothers appear, they stand in line like everyone else.

But Joseph recognizes them.

And they don't recognize him.

That's the kind of God we serve—He won't let you look like what you've been through. You've cried, been betrayed, lied on, abandoned, and left in pits—and yet, He'll clothe you in such favor and transformation that even those who hurt you won't be able to recognize the version of you God raised up.

What struck me deeply was this: the brothers were angry about a dream in which Joseph was shown reigning over them. They were enraged at the idea that Joseph would one day rise. But they didn't know—God's dream for

Joseph was so much bigger. They were worried about him ruling over their small circle.

God intended for him to rule a nation.

Can I tell you something?

People are intimidated by a piece of your dream, and they haven't even seen the full vision God has for your life.

That's why you can't stop dreaming. You can't stop pushing. You can't get discouraged when others don't understand you. They don't see the palace—only the coat. Joseph didn't retaliate. He didn't retreat. He didn't even try to go home. He trusted the process.

And wherever he found himself—a pit, a house, a prison, or a palace—he made the best of it. He didn't complain. He didn't quit. He didn't allow bitterness to take root. He stayed faithful, and God used every single step to get him to his destiny.

That's what we need to remind ourselves: every step we've taken, every betrayal we've survived, every detour we didn't ask for—it all has purpose. Together, as we walk this path, we find strength in each other's stories, recognizing the shared experiences that have shaped us. The journey may not always be easy, but embracing it with a sense of community can illuminate the purpose behind the struggles. God is using it to shape, strengthen, and prepare you. Sometimes you'll pray and not hear back. Sometimes you'll feel like you're on an island all by yourself.

Sometimes you'll wonder, "God, where are You?"

But you have to trust that His silence is not absence. His delays are not denials. And His process is not punishment—it's preparation. Joseph's story is a testimony that being given up is not the end—it's a divine setup.

# Section II —
# The Journey: Purpose Through Process

# Chapter 2:
# Given Up to Be Positioned

I come from what many would call a dysfunctional family. The truth is, the dysfunction didn't start with me—it traveled through generations. My mother's mother, my biological grandmother, battled alcoholism her entire life. I never met her, but the stories painted a picture of a woman whose pain seeped into every corner of her existence. Her relationship with my grandfather didn't last; he remarried, and the man I grew up calling "Granddaddy" wasn't biologically tied to me at all. I didn't find this out until a year before he passed away. I spent my entire childhood believing he was blood, when in reality, he was a man who stepped up and raised my mother as his own.

I do not know the full intricacies of my mother's childhood—those details remain locked behind doors she never opened. But trauma has a way of leaving fingerprints long after the moment has passed. Somewhere between her upbringing, the instability of her home, and the pain she carried, life took her down roads lined with brokenness, including drugs and things unspoken.

Growing up, she never told me about the family beyond the one sister I knew. I discovered through Ancestry years later that there were other siblings she never mentioned. She also never told me that the man I thought was her father was actually her stepfather. Secrets had settled over our family like dust in a room no one wanted disturbed.

On top of that, my mother had four children by four different fathers. That alone created its own instability and confusion about identity. I didn't meet my own biological father until I was a preteen, but when I did, there was no resentment or hostility. He walked into my life and became the best father I could have ever asked for. God knows how to redeem time.

"I will restore to you the years that the locust has eaten . . ."—Joel 2:25, KJV.

But before any of that restoration, before I understood anything about destiny, my story almost took an entirely different direction.

When I was born, drugs were found in my mother's system. The hospital and the authorities were prepared to take me away and place me into the system. With fear and desperation rising, my mother began calling around, trying to find someone—anyone—who would take me long enough to keep me out of foster care.

Years later, I learned that she even reached out to my oldest brother—twenty years my senior—who was serving in the military at the time. But the communication never reached him directly. It was intercepted by someone connected to him, and the plan stalled.

But God already had a better plan.

My biological mother had a close friend—someone who ran in the same circles with her during that season—who somehow learned what was happening. She confronted my mother and said:

"Girl, why didn't you tell me you were losing your baby?

I have an aunt who would be honored to take care of your child."

And it was at that moment that God rewrote the script.

The hospital called the woman who would become my mother—the woman God assigned—and asked her one simple question:

"How soon can you be at the hospital with a car seat?"

Four days after I entered this world, I entered purpose.

I entered safety.

I entered destiny.

I entered divine alignment.

From four days old until now, I have been right where God wanted me to be. But being given up—even when God is in it—comes with emotional weight. Heavyweight. As a child, when you are given up, it raises questions you don't have answers for. I remember one particular night when the weight of these questions felt unbearable. I was lying in bed, staring at the ceiling, wondering why I wasn't wanted. Thoughts whirled in my mind: Was it something I did? Was there a flaw in me that others could see but I couldn't? In the stillness of the night, every tick of the clock seemed to whisper doubts, and every shadow seemed to deepen my loneliness. I longed for answers, for a reason that could explain why I felt like an outsider in my own story. These were the nights that made the emotional weight tangible, nights that lingered in the corners of my heart, demanding answers that were slow to arrive.

Why wasn't I wanted?

Why wasn't I enough?

Why me?

Why couldn't she raise me?

Why was I the one given away?

Even though I maintained a relationship with my biological mother, the inconsistency cut deep. She would say she was coming to see me . . . and wouldn't show up. She would promise to pick me up . . . and never arrive. The sound of a car pulling up outside the house sent me running to the door—hoping maybe this time it was her.

Most times . . . it wasn't.

I would call her phone, and it would go unanswered. She would promise she was on the way . . . and never come. Each broken promise felt like reliving the same rejection. The same abandonment. The same wound.

There were nights I dreamed about the hurt and woke up with my pillow soaked in tears. There were years when I couldn't talk about any of it without crying. And I've learned that:

"Hope deferred makes the heart sick . . ."
—Proverbs 13:12, NLT

People like to say, "Rejection is God's protection."

But when you're drowning in rejection, that phrase doesn't feel like comfort. It feels like a cliché from a place you haven't yet matured into.

Because nobody wants to feel unwanted. Nobody wants to feel unloved. Nobody wants to feel abandoned.

My identity struggled because my sense of belonging did. I tried to fit in spaces never built for me. I adapted my behavior to feel accepted. I was introduced to things I had no business being around, just trying to be included. My relationships with women were shaped through the broken lens of my upbringing. I tried balancing multiple relationships, not because I was confident, but because I didn't trust love to last.

Emotionally, socially, academically—I struggled. I remember coming close to being kicked out of school twice. I didn't realize it then, but unhealed hurt in one area will always leak into other areas. Hurt shows up. Pain resurfaces. Trauma spills.

But everything changed in the summer of 2014.

By then, I was already in ministry, preaching and leading. Yet it was in that season that God opened my eyes to something I had never fully grasped:

I wasn't just given up.

I was given up on purpose.

In 2014, God showed me the divine thread, the intentional path, the unseen protection. I realized that if I had not been given up . . .

if I had not been adopted . . .

if I had remained where I was born . . .

I would not know God the way I know Him today.

And God taught me something powerful:

The wound of their leaving was less dangerous than the damage of their staying.

There is nothing pleasant about rejection, abandonment, separation, divorce, heartbreak, or broken promises. None of that feels good. But sometimes God removes the wrong people so He can send the right ones.

A dear sister of mine and I often remind each other:

Sometimes God has to break your heart in order to save your soul.

It is better to hurt for a season and let the wrong people walk away than to hold onto them and experience a lifetime of damage.

Being given up put me in the hands of the one God called to raise me. She wasn't just a caretaker—she was nurturing a world changer, developing a destiny shaker, shaping a vessel God intended to use.

"You intended to harm me, but God intended it all for good . . ."—Genesis 50:20, NLT

What I went through also taught me something else:

You must give up your right to hurt in order to receive healing.

I had every reason to be hurt, bitter, unforgiving, and angry. What happened to me was not my fault. But the healing was my responsibility. Consider this: What would giving up that right open for you? By releasing the grip on hurt, you invite hope, peace, and the possibility of a transformed future.

Holding onto hurt would never heal me. Replaying rejection would never restore me. And while I was rehearsing old wounds, the person who caused them was living their life, unaffected by the pain they caused.

So I ask you:

What is holding you hostage?

What hurt has paralyzed your forward movement?

What pain has stretched so deep that it surpassed even the grave, where the one who hurt you is dead and gone, yet you still carry the weight?

Purpose is often birthed in pain, but it is shaped in nurture.

God didn't just redirect me.

God repositioned me.

God aligned me.

God planted me in the place where purpose could be cultivated, and destiny could be nurtured.

I wasn't just given up.

I was given over to God's plan, God's timing, and God's destiny for my life. As the years unfolded, I began to see that every tear, every disappointment, every moment of abandonment was not wasted. God was shaping me, molding me, and preparing me for something far greater than I could imagine. My life was not the result of chance or circumstance. It was the result of a divine orchestration—a God who sees the end from the beginning and positions us exactly where we need to be.

And as I grew, healed, and walked into the calling on my life, I came to understand something even deeper:

Purpose doesn't start when life becomes easy.

Purpose starts in the places where life breaks you.

What began as a painful beginning was becoming a purposeful becoming.

And that revelation . . .

that awakening . . .

that divine shift . . .

. . . is what leads us into Chapter Three.

# Chapter 3: Called From What Should Have Crushed You

I often think about the image of a child playing with a toy—smiling, laughing, lost in their own world—until, suddenly, the toy breaks. And the moment it breaks, the child loses interest. What once brought joy becomes something to abandon, something to toss aside for something newer, shinier, better.

The truth is, nobody likes broken things.

Nobody goes out searching for something damaged, saying, "Let me buy this broken thing and see if I can put it back together." We admire what is whole. We invest in what looks functional. Brokenness doesn't attract—it repels.

But somebody once said something that caught on years ago, and it stuck with me:

"Even broken crayons still color."

And I've lived long enough to know that things that are broken often become things that are blessed—when they are placed in the right hands.

It was evident early in my life that I struggled with feelings of abandonment. There is a bond between a boy and his mother, unlike anything else. And no matter how much I told myself I was fine . . . no matter how much I tried to deny it . . . . There was a little boy inside of me, craving acceptance and longing to belong to the one who gave me birth.

I wrestled with promises made and not kept. I struggled with people saying one thing and doing another. I wrestled with the internal fear that everyone I loved would eventually leave. And as I said in the earlier chapters, I was on my way to becoming a womanizer—shaping unhealthy behaviors in relationships—all rooted in fear, abandonment, and insecurity.

We often analyze the fruit of a person's life without ever asking about the root. We see the promiscuity, the anger, the alcohol, the attitude, the self-sabotage, the rebellion—but rarely do we pause long enough to ask why. Ninety-nine percent of the time, the "why" is buried beneath a pain nobody sees and a story nobody knows.

And yet, through everything I endured, God kept me emotionally and spiritually. I was not a statistic. I did not fall into many of the traps that claim the lives of children who grew up the way I did.

God may not always omit you from the struggle,

but He will always keep you in the battle.

Consider the woman in Scripture with the issue of blood. For twelve long years, she suffered, bled, hemorrhaged. Scripture says:

". . . she had suffered a great deal under the care of many doctors . . . yet instead of getting better she grew worse."—Mark 5:26, NLT

She was not healed during those years. She wasn't delivered during those years. God did not prevent her from going through it. But God preserved her in it. Truth be told, she had lost enough blood to die eight times over.

Yet she lived.

And that's the story for so many of us. You didn't skip the storm. You didn't bypass the pain.

You didn't avoid the heartbreak. But God sustained you. God carried you. God kept you alive long enough to touch Jesus.

Sometimes, what we call misery is actually the birthplace of ministry.

Before I ever knew my calling, before I ever preached a sermon, before I ever held a microphone, God had already begun nurturing a purpose inside me. And it began at home—with the mother God gave me.

I grew up watching my mother live the life she talked about. She wasn't holy in public and hellish in private. She was the same person in the kitchen as she was in the sanctuary. Many mornings, I woke up to the sound of her praying and singing on her knees before the Lord. Something in me was drawn to those moments. I would follow the sound, kneel beside her, and join her in prayer.

I loved church—everything about it. I loved the choir, the musicians, the directors, the altar workers, and above all, the preacher. I would come home from church and have full services by myself. I would preach. I would sing. I would play on my instruments. And I often did this outside on the porch.

People would stop and listen. Cars would pull over. Neighbors would come outside, sit, and watch. I will never forget the man across the street who, so moved, told my mother that one day, he went to the back porch and cried. He told her, "Whatever you're doing, keep doing it—because it's working."

But even with all of that, I ran from my calling.

When I realized what God was doing in my life, I tried to fight it. I tried to do every damnable thing I could think of to make God change His mind about me.

Little did I know:

"God is not a man that He should lie, neither the son of man that He should repent . . ."—Numbers 23:19, KJV

In other words, He won't change His mind about you.

Not because of your mistakes.

Not because of your insecurities.

Not because of your running.

So, when people ask me, "Why ministry? Why the call?"

I tell them, I didn't choose it—God called me from what should have crushed me.

Shaped by abandonment.

Refined in rejection.

Pressed in silence.

Formed in adversity.

Yet protected by purpose.

Growing up, I was teased, talked about, and criticized. Negative words were spoken over my life by people who should have nurtured me. Early in ministry, I was omitted from programs because someone said, "All he's going to do is cry." Others said I would never be anything, never amount to anything.

But long before anyone had an opinion about me, God had a plan for me.

There were seasons when ministry discouraged me. Seasons where I was accused of doing too much.

Seasons where people grew critical of my decisions. Seasons where it felt like nothing was happening—no invitations, no engagements, no open doors.

I experienced seasons of total silence:

Praying . . . but no answer.

Crying out . . . but no response.

Speaking to God . . . but hearing nothing back.

But I learned a valuable truth: Silence can be a fertile ground for spiritual perseverance. You can't let the silence of the season shut down your productivity in the season. When God is silent, you hold on to what He already told you until He speaks again. Because no season is wasted. No season is pointless. No season is without purpose. Remember, when the heavens seem quiet, a faithful heart can still flourish.

Sometimes life gets noisy.

The storm gets loud.

The waves get violent.

The winds get boisterous.

Just like that night on the Sea of Galilee (Mark 4:35–41). The disciples panicked because the storm's noise drowned out their faith. But Jesus was still in the boat. Still present. Still in control.

Never allow the noise of the storm to drown out the voice of the Savior.

Because He said:

"My sheep know My voice . . ."—John 10:27, KJV

Pain is not absent from purpose.

Pain is part of your preparation.

David said:

"It was good for me that I was afflicted; that I might learn thy statutes."—Psalm 119:71, KJV

Pain teaches obedience.

Pain gives clarity.

Pain births identity.

God brings everything full circle.

Just like how my biological mother's friend—who stepped in the moment I needed rescuing—was connected to the very family God would later use to anchor my destiny. There are some connections you won't understand until later. Some intersections you won't appreciate until time reveals them.

There is glory in your grief.

God never wastes pain.

And sometimes, the very thing that tried to crush you becomes the thing God uses to call you.

As I matured—emotionally, spiritually, and in ministry—I learned that purpose isn't discovered in perfect places. It is unearthed in brokenness, cultivated in adversity, and matured in storms. What was meant to crush me ended up calling me. What tried to break me ended up building me. What threatened to drown me taught me how to breathe underwater.

And that understanding sets the stage for what comes next.

Because before you can embrace destiny . . .

before you can carry the weight of calling . . .

you must confront and conquer the identity shaped by your pain.

# Chapter 4: Saved by Surrender

There arose a new king in Egypt— a king who knew not Joseph. The generation that benefitted from Joseph's leadership, his wisdom, his stewardship, and his God-given strategy had died. And with the death of Joseph's generation came the death of institutional memory.

Egypt forgot who blessed them.

Egypt forgot who preserved them.

Egypt forgot what God did through Joseph.

And in forgetting Joseph, they misjudged Israel.

Scripture says the new king looked at the children of Israel and told his people,

"Behold, the children of Israel are more and mightier than we."—Exodus 1:9, KJV.

Doesn't that sound familiar?

Some people feel threatened not because you've done anything to them, but simply because of the potential they see in you. Sometimes the intimidation doesn't come from your actions—but from your anointing.

Pharaoh set out to stop Israel from multiplying.

He wanted control. Population control. Future control.

He wanted to limit, restrict, and suppress them.

But somebody once said,

"We don't die, we multiply."

Pharaoh placed taskmasters over them to afflict them.

He enslaved God's people to build treasure cities for him.

He tried to break them through labor, crush them through work, and weaken them through oppression.

But the Bible says something powerful:

"But the more they afflicted them, the more they multiplied and grew."—Exodus 1:12, KJV

No matter what system was created to stop them, God's favor was greater than Pharaoh's fear. And the same is true in your life:

There are things that were designed to break you—but couldn't.

Designed to crush you—but didn't.

Designed to stop your future—but failed.

You are the comeback kid.

You may bend.

You may sway.

You may rock.

But you cannot be broken.

The Egyptians made Israel serve "with rigor." The word "rigor" comes from a root meaning to break in pieces or crush. That's what the enemy wants—to break you in pieces, to crush your spirit, disrupt your identity, and destroy your destiny.

But no matter how intense the pressure, when God is for you, it doesn't matter who stands against you (Romans 8:31).

Pharaoh grew desperate. He summoned the Hebrew midwives and commanded them:

If a Hebrew woman gives birth to a boy, kill him.

If it's a girl, let her live.

The attack on the male seed is not new.

It has always been about the seed carriers —the carriers of destiny, lineage, identity, and legacy.

But the midwives feared God more than they feared Pharaoh. And because they feared God, they refused to participate in genocide. They delayed. They avoided. They strategically

"Arrived too late."

Pharaoh escalated the attack.

He commanded that every newborn

Hebrew boy be thrown into the Nile River.

What Pharaoh meant for destruction,

God intended for direction.

The same river that was assigned to kill

Moses

would be the river that carried him to his

purpose.

THE MOTHER WHO SURRENDERED:

Jochebed's Painful Purpose

Moses' parents—Jochebed and Amram—

gave birth to a son and hid him for three months.

Moses is one of the rare figures in Scripture

whose life is sketched from the womb to the tomb. His story begins in danger and moves into destiny.

When Jochebed could no longer hide him, she built a basket—an ark—sealed with the same kind of material used to waterproof Noah's ark. She placed her baby in the Nile and surrendered him into God's hands.

Sometimes God requires you to surrender the thing you love most to preserve the thing, He designed it to become.

Sometimes God has to break your heart to save your soul.

Sometimes God will ask you to do something uncomfortable, painful, and confusing—not because He wants to hurt you, but because there is a bigger picture at play.

Jochebed let Moses go . . .

but she let him go into the hands of God.

THE PROVIDENCE OF GOD:

Perfect Timing, Perfect Positioning

Pharaoh's daughter "just so happened" to come down to bathe at the river at the exact time Moses floated by.

But there are no coincidences in God.

The Spirit of God timed the place, the person, and the progress.

The princess saw the basket, opened it, and the baby cried—and compassion rose in her heart.

Moses' sister Miriam, following the basket from a distance, stepped forward at the perfect moment, and offered to find a Hebrew woman to nurse the baby.

And who did she bring?

Jochebed—Moses' own mother.

Pharaoh's daughter unknowingly paid Moses' mother from Pharaoh's treasury to raise the very child Pharaoh ordered to kill.

Only God can write irony like that.

God will cause your enemy to fund your future.

God will cause your adversary to do a favor for you.

God will turn what was meant to destroy you into the thing that develops you.

Jochebed gave Moses up to save him— and in doing so, she positioned him for purpose.

He was abandoned to protect him.

He was released to preserve him.

He was surrendered to save a nation.

## A PRINCE WITH A SLAVE'S HEART:

Identity Crisis and Divine Calling

Moses grew up in luxury.

He was educated, trained, and equipped in the finest systems of Egypt. He lived in privilege . . . but carried an ache that only adopted children understand.

Acts 7:22–23 says Moses was "mighty in words and deeds" and fully trained in Egyptian wisdom.

Yet he wrestled with his identity.

He was raised as an Egyptian . . .

but born as a Hebrew.

He lived in a palace . . .

but belonged to a people in chains.

Sometimes you don't fit because God is preparing you to leave.

Sometimes you feel the friction because your season is changing.

Sometimes your spirit grows restless because your destiny is calling.

Moses embraced his true identity:

He was a son of Abraham, not a son of Pharaoh.

Hebrews 11 says he chose to suffer with God's people rather than enjoy the pleasures of Egypt for a season. Purpose was pulling him. Destiny was drawing him. He was called to something bigger than royalty.

## THE MISSTEP THAT MOVED HIM: When God Uses Your Mistakes

Moses saw an Egyptian beating a Hebrew slave.

He had witnessed this kind of injustice countless times.

But this time he erupted.

He intervened.

He killed the Egyptian and buried him in the sand.

People argue over whether Moses was defending or murdering. Regardless, this is true:

Moses acted prematurely,

but God still used him powerfully.

One wrong move didn't cancel his calling.

One mistake didn't void his destiny.

His error didn't eliminate God's plan.

The next day, two Hebrews were fighting. Moses stepped in, and one said,

"Will you kill me like you killed the Egyptian?"

Moses realized his secret wasn't a secret.

Pharaoh sought to kill him.

Moses fled to Midian.

Rejected by Egypt.

Rejected by the Hebrews.

Rejected by Pharaoh.

Rejected by people.

But accepted by God.

THE WILDERNESS THAT MOLDED HIM

Moses entered Midian as a fugitive but emerged as a shepherd.

He traded the palace for pasture.

He exchanged luxury for obscurity.

He surrendered influence for isolation.

But God was shaping him.

Many times, God will take you to a place you've never been to prepare you for a purpose you've never seen.

Moses needed the wilderness because God would later call him to lead Israel through that same wilderness. Your wilderness is not punishment — It is preparation.

And while Moses was wandering, confused, rejected, abandoned . . .

God was molding him.

Preparing him.

Deconstructing Egypt from his identity and depositing destiny into his spirit.

Jochebed did not surrender Moses because she didn't love him.

She surrendered him because she did.

She surrendered him so God could save him.

She surrendered him so God could position him.

She surrendered him so God could raise a deliverer.

Sometimes God requires painful releases because the destiny He has for you cannot be developed in the place you are trying to remain.

Moses was abandoned to save his life.

Moses was raised in Pharaoh's house to confront Pharaoh.

Moses was rejected by his own people to rely on God.

Moses was sent to the wilderness to learn leadership.

Rejection was protection.

Abandonment was alignment.

Surrender was salvation.

Moses' life teaches us that purpose is often birthed in unusual places—in rivers, in palaces, in deserts, in mistakes, and in moments of surrender. His story shows us that God uses flawed, fearful, uncertain people for extraordinary assignments.

But Moses' journey doesn't stop at survival.

It continues into the realm of calling— where God interrupts his wilderness with fire, with voice, with purpose. And maturity has caused me to recognize something that I could not see when I was younger.

Whatever the reasoning was that brought me to where I am today, it had to unfold the way it did. I no longer wrestle with the "why" the way I once did. I no longer sit in confusion about how my story began. I have come to understand that what felt like abandonment was actually orchestration.

The best thing my biological mother could have done for me was surrender me.

Not because she did not love me.

But because there was a destiny on my life that required a different environment to shape it.

While I was living through it, I was too close to it to understand it. Pain has a way of blurring perspective. When you are inside the story, you cannot always see the hand of God writing it.

As a child, I could not reconcile the separation.

As a young man, I wrestled with the rejection.

But as a mature man, I see the sovereignty.

What I once labeled loss, heaven labeled alignment.

What I once called abandonment, God called protection.

What I once questioned, God had already ordained.

It was not random.

It was not careless.

It was not a mistake.

It was God-orchestrated.

And the same way Moses was placed in a palace to confront a king, I was placed in the right hands to shape the man I would become. The surrender that looked painful was the very thing that positioned me for purpose.

Some destinies require distance.

Some callings require separation.

Some futures demand surrender.

And when I look back now, I do not see a broken beginning.

I see divine strategy.

# Chapter 5: Purpose After Failure

Have you ever reached a place in your life where you felt like you had given up on yourself? Perhaps you suffered a public failure.

Maybe you repeatedly made the same mistakes.

Maybe you found yourself back in a place you swore you would never be again.

That moment—when disappointment meets exhaustion—is dangerous. Not because

God has left us, but because we often abandon ourselves there.

Purpose can be defined as the object toward which one strives or for which something exists. It speaks to intention, aim, and the desired end God saw before we ever took our first breath. Most of us would agree that we were created on purpose, with purpose, and for purpose. Because of this, we must come to a resolution: we are not going through anything without reason. Even our darkest days and heaviest moments are woven into the fabric of God's plan, pushing us one step closer to our expected end.

If we could have it our way, we would all reach for a get-out-of-the-process-free card—something like the get-out-of-jail-free card in the game of Monopoly. But purpose does not work like that. Purpose requires process, and process always includes pain.

Pain is often the indication that something is shifting. Pain whispers, You're closer to purpose than you think. Pain and suffering, in fact, suggest that you are doing something right. Scripture reminds us, "Think it not strange concerning the fiery trial which is to try you." (1 Peter 4:12).

When you understand purpose, you begin to appreciate the process. And when you know your purpose, the things that once made you cry will not break you the same way anymore.

It is here that I would like to introduce you to a man named Peter.

Before he was an apostle, before he preached on the Day of Pentecost, before he became a pillar of the church, he was simply a fisherman.

One day, Jesus was teaching by the Lake of Gennesaret. He noticed two empty boats along the shore and fishermen washing their nets—cleaning up, packing up, and preparing to go home. Jesus stepped into Peter's boat, sat down, and taught the crowd from the water. When He finished, He turned to Peter and said, "Launch out into the deep and let down your nets for a catch."

Peter responded honestly—and exhaustedly: "Master, we have toiled all night and caught nothing. Nevertheless, at Your word, I will let down the net."

Have you ever felt like a failure?

Have you ever tried your best and still come up empty?

Have you ever washed your nets mentally, emotionally, or spiritually—because you were ready to give up?

Peter obeyed to an extent anyway. Suddenly, the net began to break, and boats began to sink because of the abundance of fish. This is where we begin to see Peter's humanity, and this is where we learn that purpose does not require perfection—it requires obedience. Peter had strong faith. Jesus renamed him (Simon), Cephas —Peter—meaning rock. He helped choose a replacement for Judas. He healed a man crippled from birth with the words, "Silver and gold have I none, but such as I have give I unto thee." Crowds believed even his shadow could heal. The Apostle Paul later referred to him as a pillar of the church.

But pillars can crack.

Rocks can crumble.

And even those who walk closest with Jesus can wrestle with insecurity.

This same Peter cut off a soldier's ear. This same Peter walked on water—and then began to sink. This same Peter swore he would never leave Jesus.

At the Last Supper, when Jesus revealed that one of them would betray Him, an argument broke out among the disciples about who was the greatest. Right in the middle of that debate, Jesus looked directly at Peter and said, "Simon, Simon, Satan has desired to have you, that he may sift you as wheat. But I have prayed for you, that your faith fails not. And when you are converted, strengthen your brothers."

Jesus was speaking a language Peter understood.

Sifting was a familiar process in Peter's world. Wheat was never useful straight from the field. Before it could become bread, it had to be shaken, separated, and passed through a sieve. The purpose of sifting was not to destroy the wheat—it was to separate what was valuable from what was useless. The chaff was light, empty, and easily blown away. The wheat, however, was weighty. It remained.

So, when Jesus said Satan desired to sift Peter, He was not saying the enemy wanted to kill him. He was saying the enemy wanted to shake him, expose him, and pressure him, hoping that when the shaking was over, nothing of value would remain.

Sifting reveals what is real.

Under pressure, what is shallow falls away. What is rooted stays. That is why sifting feels violent—it attacks confidence, identity, and self-belief. It makes you question whether what you carry is strong enough to survive the shaking.

And here is the part we often miss: Jesus did not stop the sifting.

He allowed it.

But He added something crucial: "I have prayed for you, that your faith fail not."

Jesus did not pray that Peter would avoid failure.

He prayed that Peter would survive it.

Peter was not being sifted because he was weak. He was being sifted because he was chosen. The enemy has a way of targeting purposeful individuals. God allowed the shaking because there were things in Peter that could not go forward into leadership—pride, self- confidence, comparison, and an overestimation of his own strength. Peter believed he was strong enough to stand on his own. The sifting would teach him dependence.

That very night, Peter failed publicly—and repeatedly. He folded under pressure. He denied knowing Jesus not once, not twice, but three times. His mouth betrayed his heart.

And if we are honest, many of us know exactly what that feels like.

We love God, and yet there are moments when we still disappoint Him.

We love Him deeply, but our actions don't always reflect our devotion.

Our hearts may be sincere, but somehow, we still make a mess of things.

Peter didn't deny Jesus because he stopped believing in Him. He denied Him because fear began to drown out his faith. And if we are honest with ourselves, who among us has the right to judge Peter? Many of us never stopped loving the Lord—we just became quiet when it mattered most. We didn't walk away from Him; we simply learned how to blend in, because standing out felt too expensive, too risky, and too costly for where we were at the time.

What makes Peter's failure even more painful is how close he was to Jesus. This was not ignorance. This was not even distance. Peter knew Him. He walked with Him. He saw the miracles.

He was part of the inner circle. And still . . . he failed.

After Jesus was arrested, Peter followed at a distance. Three confrontations. Three denials.

Pressure exposed the hidden parts of him—the part afraid of being seen as weak, the part that wanted belonging more than obedience. And in that moment, Peter did not just deny Jesus—he gave up on himself.

When the rooster crowed, Peter remembered Jesus' words and ran away in shame. Just like earlier, when he washed his nets, Peter believed his story was over.

Comparison played a role, too. Comparison is a thief of joy. When you compare your process to someone else's, you are really saying you want their journey—including their suffering. Every destiny has a price.

Peter was ready to quit because he assumed failure was final. And many of us feel the same way.

Maybe you did not finish school.

Maybe you lost your job.

Maybe you were unfaithful.

Maybe you lied, cheated, hurt someone, or made a decision you regret.

But failure is not final when God is still calling your name.

Jesus saw another version of Peter—one Peter had never met yet. A bold Peter. A restored Peter. A Spirit-filled Peter. A world-changing Peter. And the same is true for you. There is a version of you that you have not met yet.

I shared earlier how, in my younger years, when it was evident that God's calling was on my life, I tried to run from it. I intentionally did things—damnable things—hoping God would change His mind about using me. What I did not realize then was that the gifts and callings of God is without repentance. Purpose is stronger than failure.

Jesus did not confront Peter immediately. He allowed him to sit with it. After the resurrection, Jesus asked Peter one question—not Why did you deny me? Not, how could you embarrass me? Not, can I still trust you?

He asked, "Do you love me?"

Three times.

The same number of times Peter denied Him.

Jesus was not trying to shame Peter—He was restoring him at the point of his failure. Peter's failure did not cancel his calling. Jesus did not disqualify him, replace him, or revoke his assignment.

Some of us think it is over because we failed under pressure. But God is saying that failure Did not cancel your assignment—it was part of its fulfillment.

Peter became the leader he was because he knew what it felt like to fall and still be loved.

He could preach grace because he had needed it. He could shepherd others because he had been shepherded.

Peter denied publicly. Jesus restored him publicly. And on the Day of Pentecost, Peter stepped into his finest hour. The same man who once denied Jesus now stood boldly and declared, "These are not drunk as you suppose . . . this is that which was spoken by the prophet Joel." Three thousand souls were saved.

The same Peter who quit.

The same Peter who failed.

The same Peter who denied Him—preached revival.

Peter's story teaches us that growth often includes failure, but failure does not disqualify you—it develops you. Peter had a grace that would not allow his future to be canceled.

Peter may have given up on himself, but God never did.

And neither has He given up on you.

# Section III —
# The Revelation: Purpose Unlocked

# Chapter 6: The Purpose of Being Given Up

What if every detour is a divine strategy? I have never been one to believe in accidents or happenstance. I believe that everything happens on purpose for a purpose. We serve a God of intentionality. "Oops" is not in His vocabulary. Everything He does, He does for a reason—and for a purpose that is often far beyond our comprehension and understanding. Scripture reminds us that His ways are not our ways, and His thoughts are higher than our thoughts. God is a God of strategy. He has a strategic way of bringing to pass the things He has in store for our lives. And sometimes, if we're honest, it feels like God takes the long way, the harder way, the not-so-easy way to get us to our place of destiny. There are things in life that may seem accidental: Accidentally signing up for the wrong major. Accidentally applying for the wrong job.

Accidentally going the wrong way or showing up at the wrong place. But sometimes those moments are not as accidental as we think. They are part of God's strategy. When I consider my own life, it often feels like one in a million. Children are given up for adoption all the time, yet when you're the one living the story, it can feel hopeless, confusing, and deeply personal. I dealt with feelings of rejection and abandonment, low self-worth, jealousy—especially toward my siblings who were raised by my biological mother. There were so many questions I could not answer. But something shifted in me when my biological grandfather said, "Not being raised by your birth mother had to be one of the best things that could have ever happened to you."

That statement confirmed what God had already begun to show me: sometimes you are better off with a person's absence than you would be with their presence. Unfortunately, my siblings, who were raised by my biological mother, faced different challenges, struggles, and addictions. I don't say that to judge or blame them. They were simply playing the hand they were dealt. But I am a firm believer that although the hurt and the pain may not be our fault, the healing and the recovery are our responsibility.

Growing up, I wanted so badly to have a relationship with my birth mother. I could not understand why I was the one given up. Why was I the one adopted? Why was I treated differently? But now, looking back, I see that it was necessary. Because if I had not been given up, if I had not been adopted, if I had not experienced what I experienced, I would not know God the way I know Him today. People releasing you often reveal God's hand selecting you. I think about David. When the prophet Samuel came to Jesse's house to anoint the next king of Israel, all of David's brothers were present—but David wasn't even invited. Son after son passed before Samuel, but the horn of oil would not pour. Finally,

Samuel asked, "Do you have any more sons?" Jesse replied that there was one more—the shepherd boy. The overlooked one. The disregarded one. The pretty boy in the field. And that was the one God chose. People may overlook you, but you are not overlooked by God. The Bible says, "When my mother and my father forsake me, then the Lord will take me up." Maybe you feel like you come from an unusable situation. Maybe you were adopted. Maybe you were given up. Maybe you've battled anxiety or depression. Maybe you've made mistakes. Maybe you've been an adulterer, a liar, a cheater, an abuser, or the abused. None of that disqualifies you from God's purpose.

Oftentimes, the reason we are fought so hard is because the enemy knows what we're becoming. If he can stop you now, he can interrupt who you are destined to be. Sometimes God will place you in a situation and cut off every visible source of support. People will see what you're going through. Some will even have the power to help—but they won't. Not because God has abandoned you, but because if they rescue you, you might give them the credit instead of God. Abandonment creates a storm of emotions. It makes you feel isolated. Forgotten. Unwanted. The haunting question becomes: Why wasn't I enough? Why wasn't I enough to make you change? Why wasn't I enough to make you fight harder? Why wasn't I enough to make you stay? But here is the truth: You are enough. When God finished creating everything, He looked at what He had made and declared it good—including you. Many figures in Scripture experienced abandonment. David. Joseph. Job. Moses. Elijah. Even Jesus felt forsaken on the cross.

Yet Hebrews 13:5 reminds us that God will never leave us nor forsake us. God is not only a present help in trouble—He is a pleasant help. Elijah was exhausted and depressed, and God fed him and let him rest before speaking to him. Moses felt rejected, but God used him to deliver a nation. Job lost everything, but God restored double. Joseph was thrown into a pit, but ended up in a palace. David was hunted, but eventually crowned. Jesus was crucified—but rose with all power. And I was given up—but God gave me a family, a future, and a purpose. Sometimes what feels like rejection is actually redirection. I didn't choose to be given up. I didn't choose to be adopted. But God turned what happened to me into something that worked in my favor. Being given up was not the end of my story. It was the beginning of my calling. Statistically, I should be addicted. I should be broken. I should be lost. But I am not a statistic. I am a child of purpose.

Reflection & Application

Where in your life did you interpret redirection as rejection?

What if the very thing that hurt you was the thing God used to position you?

Can you begin thanking God not only for what He did—but also for what He did not allow?

Purpose Declaration

What tried to break me only built me.

What tried to bury me only planted me.

I was not rejected—I was redirected.

# Chapter 7: Pray for the Me That Nobody Knows

Someone once asked, "Where do the broken hearts go?" Scripture answers it plainly: "When my heart is overwhelmed, lead me to the rock that is higher than I." (Psalm 61:2) But I want to ask a different question. Where do gifted people go when their hearts are overwhelmed? Where do you go when you're strong for everyone else—but secretly tired? Where do you go when people celebrate your gift—but never check on your soul? Where do you go when you are applauded in public, but bleeding in private? Where do gifted individuals go to be cultivated, not just used? Where are the support groups for people who carry weight that most people can't see? Where are the safe spaces for those who are anointed, talented, called—and still human? How do these gifts get stirred, nurtured, and developed when the person carrying them is silently breaking? Because the truth is, many gifted people live lonely lives. And often, the loneliest people in the room are the ones everyone thinks are the strongest.

Many times, gifted individuals live lonely lives. Even though we may have many friends and be surrounded by many people, we can still feel isolated—often misunderstood and mischaracterized. There are certain elements about our gifting and our walk that we don't even understand ourselves. Gifted people are often judged for their gifts rather than truly welcomed in many circles. There are so many battles that gifted individuals go through that many people never see: bouts of depression, rejection, fear, worry, being misunderstood, laughed at, and criticized. People will laugh at you because you're different, which makes it that much harder to embrace what God has placed on your life—the mere fact that you're not like everyone else. Somewhere inside many of us is an inner child still seeking affirmation—wanting to be accepted, wanted, affirmed. How many individuals do you know who stay in trouble, do things they have no business doing, compromise, and live beneath their calling—all for the sake of affirmation?

All because they want to be accepted by people who honestly don't have their best interests at heart. That inner child is still seeking affirmation and acceptance because they have not yet reached a place of comfort in their own skin. They're still trying to fit into circles that perhaps were never designed for them. Many people are not honest, especially because you cannot physically see the side effects of a broken heart. But many of us need emotional healing. We must learn to give up our right to hurt in order to receive our healing. That means what we've gone through—what we've experienced and endured—we have every reason to be angry, bitter, unforgiving, and dare I say, hateful, vengeful, and spiteful. But holding on to that right will not bring healing and wholeness. There was a point in my journey where I thought I had forgiven my birth mother and that I was over what happened to me in my childhood. But life has a way of teaching you something: sometimes we let go of things that we have not necessarily gotten over. That lesson became very real to me in 2008. At that time, I was seeking the Lord to be filled with His Holy Spirit, with the evidence of speaking in tongues.

We were approaching a three-night shut-in at my church. Before the shut-in began on that Sunday night in June, we had a youth department meeting. I was serving as the youth pastor at that time. What was supposed to be a meeting turned into what felt like a verbal attack against me. For all intents and purposes, I do not believe these two women of God—both much older than me, both with children older than me—meant any harm in

what they were trying to convey. But in that
moment, it felt like I was not being seen. The
things I was doing were being mischaracterized
and misinterpreted. It felt like I was not doing
enough—or that what I was doing was not right.
And if I am honest, it triggered something in me. I
remember leaving that meeting, staying for the
shut-in, physically present—but mentally checked
out. I was angry. I wanted to sic my mother on
them. I wanted her to tell them completely off,
because I knew she was more than capable of
doing it—at least back then, and truth be told, she
still has a little fight in her. I stayed there Sunday
night—mind gone, body present—going through
the motions all day Monday. Same thing. Totally
distracted. Thrown off course. And all of this was
happening when the whole reason I was there was

to be filled with the Spirit of God. Monday night, I went home and refreshed myself. When I got out of the shower, I began crying uncontrollably. Tears were streaming down my face like rainwater running down a window in the South during a hard storm. I literally did not know what was happening or why I was crying. But I am a firm believer that crying is therapeutic. It is a release of built-up frustration and buried emotion. Sometimes it's better to cry than to go off. Sometimes it's better to cry than to fight or say things you will later regret. I cried for a long time.

I still didn't know what God was doing—but I wanted Him to do whatever it was He was doing in me. I walked into the living room while I was still crying, and Joel Osteen happened to be on the television. He said something in that moment that encouraged me and that I have never forgotten to this day: "God is going to shut the mouths of the lions in your life." Those words were healing to me in that moment. I soon stopped crying, but I knew God had used that moment to heal me—not from something new, but from something I thought I was already healed from. I got my focus back and went back to the shut-in. But the enemy came to try to throw me off course again—this time through temptation. One of the church members who was not attending the shut-in told me I looked hungry. Now, how someone can look hungry, I will never understand. But she offered to take me to McDonald's. And if I'm honest—even though I didn't have my wallet on me because of being in the shut-in—I almost gave in. But something

turned in my stomach and told me, "You don't
need that food. Just wait on me." Later that night,
after Bible study during the shut-in, I began to
lead prayer. And the Lord filled me with the Holy
Ghost. He took control of my tongue. He purged
me. He rolled me across the floor. He filled me
with the Holy Spirit, with the evidence of
speaking in tongues. That night taught me
something I will never forget: Sometimes
unhealed pain can delay divine purpose. Perhaps
you have an aim. Perhaps you have a goal.
Perhaps you have something you are working
toward. But holding on to old hurt can be a
deterrent to what you are seeking to accomplish.

Don't delay another moment. Be healed
today. Make a decision that you want to be healed
more than you like the attention you get from

being the victim. That experience taught me something else, too: sometimes we don't realize we're still bleeding until life presses on the bruise. That's why we experience triggers. It will feel like whatever happened to us long ago is happening again for the first time. That's why I am a firm believer in praying the prayer, "Lord, search my heart," because sometimes there are things in our hearts that we didn't even know were still there. I had to learn how to stop rehearsing old hurts. I had to learn how to forgive what I had already forgiven. And I had to understand that forgiveness is an ongoing process—because I wanted the healing.

I understood that forgiveness—whether through receiving an apology or not—was crucial to my continued growth and development. I needed to heal more than I needed an apology. And there's someone reading this book right now —you're angry. You're bitter. You hate the person who harmed and hurt you. But holding on to that right to hurt will not bring healing and wholeness to your life. You must understand that sometimes you will have to forgive people who will never offer an apology—because forgiveness is for you, not the person who hurt you. You have to make the conscious decision to recover and to heal. And that means you have a responsibility. Even though what you are feeling and what you experienced is not your fault—you didn't cause it. I didn't ask to be given up, adopted, rejected, or abandoned—but I am responsible for my healing.

There was a time when I couldn't talk about what I had experienced without becoming emotional. I would have dreams about the mistreatment, and I would wake up with my pillow wet with tears. But I have learned how to keep my spirit pure through prayer. Forgiving someone who caused damage in your life—someone who was supposed to nurture and develop you—is a painful thing. But I had to come to a place where I refused to let it get into my spirit and contaminate it. I must keep a clear line of communication with the Father. I have to pray when I feel irritated. I have to pray when I feel like treating people the way they treated me. I have to pray in order to keep my spirit clean and pure. There is a scripture that encourages me that says: "Who shall ascend into the hill of the Lord? Or who shall stand in His holy place? He that has clean hands and a pure heart, who has not lifted

up his soul unto vanity."

It is in prayer that I have learned you can

receive information you cannot get anywhere else.

It is in prayer that God speaks to you. It is in

prayer that God builds you up and gives you the

strength you need. He fortifies you. He

strengthens you. He encourages you. He reminds

you that there is nothing you will go through that

you cannot conquer. I have been very candid with

the Lord, taking what I've been through to Him.

And I refuse to believe that God does not care

about me, for we are encouraged to cast our cares

upon Him, for He cares for us. And He promised

to perfect that which concerns us. God will

minister to you in the secret place. God can heal

the version of you that never had the language to

cry out. Don't be afraid to face what you've been through. Sometimes we have to be confrontational in order to overcome the challenges of our past. The Egyptians you see today, you shall see them again no more forever. The confrontational period does not have to be long and drawn out—but if you are willing to face it and deal with it today, God can free you from it for a lifetime.

# Chapter 8: When Purpose Hurts

No one tells you this part. They tell you about destiny. They tell you about calling. They tell you about purpose. But they don't tell you that purpose hurts. Somewhere along the way, many of us were taught—directly or indirectly—that if something is from God, it should feel good. That if you're walking in purpose, things should make sense, fall into place, and feel rewarding. Life teaches you otherwise. Some of the most necessary things in life are not pleasant at all. I grew up on old-school remedies—the kind you were told were "good for you" even though every part of your body resisted them. I remember having a bad upset stomach and being told to drink flower water. It tasted terrible, but it worked. I remember being sick and having to take castor oil—absolutely disgusting—but somehow it drove the sickness out. All household cures. None of them are enjoyable. None of them are delicious. All of them are effective. That's when God started speaking to me in a language I understood. I'm a baker. I love baking cakes—especially pound cakes. Key lime pound cake. Cream cheese pound cake. Honey bun cake. Pineapple cake. Are all some of my specialties.

One day, the Lord brought to mind the ingredients: flour, eggs, sugar, butter, and vanilla flavor. Then He showed me something simple and profound: None of those ingredients tastes good by themselves. No one eats raw flour. No one drinks vanilla extract straight. No one snacks on butter. And yet, when you put them together, mix them in the same bowl, place them in the oven, and give them time to do their work, something beautiful comes out. Everything that didn't taste good alone becomes wonderful together. That's when Romans 8:28 stopped being a quote and became a lens: "And we know that all things work together for the good of them that love God, to them who are the called according to His purpose."

It doesn't say all things are good. It says all things work together for good. There is a difference. There is a weight that comes with being called. A pressure. A responsibility. Some seasons will wound you. Some chapters will bruise you. Some experiences will leave marks you didn't ask for. There is nothing good about betrayal. Nothing good about church hurt. Nothing good about disappointment, failure, criticism, abandonment, or being misunderstood. And yet, God somehow weaves even these into the story He's writing. For a long time, I didn't understand that. For a long time, my own story hurt too much to look at. Being given up at birth. Being adopted. Growing up with questions that had no answers. Living with a quiet ache that never quite left. The sleepless nights. The bad dreams. The fear when the phone rang. The anxiety when someone knocked at the door. The wondering. The waiting. The unanswered questions. And then there were the leadership wounds. The church hurt. The betrayals that came from people I trusted. The moments that made me question myself, my calling, and sometimes even God. It all felt like too much. Until the summer of 2014. I can't explain it any other way except to say this: a light came on. It wasn't loud. It wasn't dramatic. It was quiet. Deep. Settling. It was the moment I finally got it. I finally understood my purpose. And because I finally understood it, what used to make me cry no longer did. All of it—the hurt, the pain, the tears, the sleepless nights, the anxiety, the waiting—I began to see it differently. I realized God had me on a very specific path. And because of the path He had chosen for my life, I had to be given up. I had to be adopted. Because if I weren't, I wouldn't know God the way I know Him today. I wouldn't be doing what I'm doing today. I wouldn't be who I am today. My pain wasn't random. It was assigned. And my purpose wasn't just for me. It was to help others who had been given up. Overlooked. Abandoned.

Rejected. Wounded. To inspire them. To coach them. To mentor them. Because there is power in a testimony. When we tell the truth about our stories, the same power that healed us gets released for someone else. Being called by God is not light work. You were called before the foundation of the world. Called before you were formed in your mother's womb. And God does not make casual decisions about destiny. Your story does not have to be perfect. You don't have to have it all together. The call is not something you can outrun. And one of the hardest truths about purpose is this: It can be lonely. Everyone who starts with you will not finish with you. Everyone is not anointed to carry what you carry. What you are built to survive might break someone else.

Some people are in your life for a reason. Some for a season. Some for a lifetime. And some are simply rocket boosters—assigned to get you to a certain altitude, but never meant to stay attached once you get there. Assigned places are often uncomfortable places. God will keep you uncomfortable—not to punish you—but to stretch you. Like the baby eagle learning to fly. The mother lifts it high and lets it go. The fall looks cruel. But she's watching. And if it can't fly yet, she will catch it. The fall is part of the training. God will disrupt your comfort if it means developing your character. There is a cost for the oil. Olives must be crushed. Grapes must be pressed. Gold must go through fire. And people must go through the process. David said, "It was good for me that I was afflicted, that I might learn Your statutes." Some of what hurt you was not meant to destroy you. It was meant to develop you. Some of what you've been through was not punishment. It was preparation. And one day, you'll realize: The pain was not in the way. The pain was the way.

# Section IV — The Manifestation: Purpose Revealed

# Chapter 9: Rising from the Pit to the Palace

Some stories begin in palaces. Mine began in a pit. Not a literal one, but a place just as real—a life shaped early by absence, uncertainty, and questions no child should have to carry. Before I ever understood words like "calling" or "destiny," I learned what it felt like to be moved, repositioned, handed from one chapter of life into another without explanation. I did not come from a line of preachers. No last name opened doors. My father was no bishop. My mother was no famous evangelist. If God was going to write something meaningful with my life, He would have to do it the way He often does—starting low and working upward. Even as a child, I felt that upward pull. I didn't just want to dress well; I wanted to dress like a preacher. After school, while other kids ran inside, I often stayed on the porch and turned it into a sanctuary. I lined up invisible congregations, opened a real Bible, and preached to nobody and everybody at the same time. I didn't know it then, but I was rehearsing for a future I didn't yet believe I deserved. But purpose doesn't erase pain. And pain has a way of leaking out sideways. In school, I was trouble. Suspensions. Calls home. Disappointed teachers.

The punishment was usually simple: no wrestling. Back when WWE was still WWF and SmackDown came on Thursday nights, that felt like a real loss. Still, I kept making the same mistakes, as if part of me was determined to prove I belonged in the pit. When I finally realized God was calling me, I didn't feel honored. I felt exposed. And afraid. So I tried to outrun it—not by leaving, but by sabotaging myself. I made choices I thought might disqualify me. If I messed up badly enough, surely God would choose someone else. I didn't yet know that heaven does not issue recalls on destiny. In 2004, I stopped running and preached my first sermon. I called it If It's Not One Thing, It's Another. I didn't realize then that I was preaching my own story. The following year, my grandmother died. Her death felt like another loss, but it became a turning point. My mother and I moved to Louisiana, into the house she had once lived in. What I thought was a relocation was really a rescue. Almost immediately, things began to change. The trouble stopped. The anger quieted. I wasn't that kid anymore. I still struggled with being late, but that was about it. I made the honor roll. Became the Spanish Student of the Year.

And then, something I still can hardly believe—I became the first student in my school's history to deliver the baccalaureate sermon to the graduating class. Without realizing it, I was climbing. But old thinking dies slowly. New city. New state. New faces. Nobody knew me. Nobody knew my story. Nobody knew I was called. And once again, I assumed that if people didn't recognize the gift, the gift must not matter. What I didn't know was that God doesn't wait for recognition to continue His work. I visited a few churches. One of them came with so many warnings that I almost stayed away. But my mother taught me never to let someone else's disappointment decide my direction. So I went. And from the first service, I knew—I was home. It didn't take long for someone to discover I was a minister. I was asked to preach a youth consecration service. Then came more invitations. Then I became a youth pastor. Then the district works. Then, there were jurisdictional opportunities. The climb continued. And one day, I found myself standing in Mason Temple in Memphis, Tennessee—behind the same pulpit where Dr. Martin Luther King Jr. preached his final "I've Been to the Mountaintop" sermon. In both 2009 and 2010, I had the privilege of speaking at Purity Day during the Church of God in Christ Women's International Convention. Ministered at Holy Convocation in St. Louis in 2010. Spoke at the AIM Convention in Birmingham in 2012. Not because I was the most impressive—but because God is faithful.

I've preached to rooms filled with thousands. I've preached to rooms with two or three. And I've learned this: palaces are not measured by crowds. They are measured by obedience. I don't believe in spiritual arrogance. I believe in divine placement. Promotion doesn't come from the east, west, or south. God is the judge. He lifts one and lowers another. Every door that has opened, I understand this: God didn't have to choose me. He could have chosen someone with a cleaner beginning. In a strange and painful way, I was overlooked by my biological mother. But I was never overlooked by God. Before anyone formed an opinion about me, God had already made His choice. I was chosen long before I was celebrated. And now, when I tell my story, people often come up to me and say, "That's my story too." "I was adopted." "I was given up." "You helped free me today." That's when I understand something deeper: The pit was not where my story ended. It was where God started writing it. And He is still in the business of taking what is given up . . . and revealing it was chosen all along.

# Chapter 10: Walking in Purpose on Purpose

For a long time, I thought purpose was something you found. Like a hidden door. Or a buried treasure. Or a single moment that suddenly explains everything. Now I know better. Purpose is not discovered accidentally. It is walked out—deliberately, daily, and often painfully—over time. Looking back over my life, I can see what I couldn't see while I was living it: nothing was random. Not the adoption. Not the detours. Not the delays. Not the disappointments. Not even the things that nearly broke me. Purpose is not only wrapped in the good things that happen to us. It is also hidden inside the things that keep us up at night. The things that make us cry. The things that frustrate us, stretch us, and sometimes wound us. It lives in the things we feel deeply. The things we do effortlessly. The things we can't stop caring about—even when it would be easier to. Purpose is not an accident. It is intentional. God does not design lives casually.

He crafts them. He shapes them. He layers experiences, relationships, losses, delays, and opportunities with more precision than we could ever imagine. What feels like an interruption is often instruction. What feels like a delay is often development. And what feels like it's happening to you is often happening for you. But purpose does not unfold without cooperation. Purpose requires obedience. Not partial obedience. Not convenient obedience. Not obedience when it makes sense. Real obedience. The kind that follows God's instructions even when the destination is unclear. The kind that resists the temptation to rewrite the plan. The kind that says, "I will not detour just because this road is uncomfortable." Every time in my life I tried to do things my own way, I complicated what God was trying to simplify. Purpose is precise. And precision demands obedience. Purpose also demands discipline.

If Joseph teaches us anything, it is this: purpose is always greater than pleasure. You cannot carry destiny and indulge in distraction at the same time. There are things you must say no to. Paths you must refuse to walk down. People you may have to love from a distance. Not because you are better—but because your assignment is bigger. Discipline is not punishment. It is protection. It protects what God is building in you before it is visible to anyone else. Purpose also requires surrender. This may be the hardest part. Because most of us don't mind trusting God with the big things. What we struggle with is giving Him control of the daily things. The decisions. The timing. The outcomes. The way it all unfolds. We like to feel in control. And control is often the enemy of trust. At some point, I had to surrender not just my fears and failures, but my need to manage the process. I had to place my disappointments, my questions, my pain, my hopes, and my future into hands wiser than my own. Purpose does not coexist with control. You have to choose one. And purpose will always call you upward. It will not allow you to stay where you are. It will interrupt your comfort. It will challenge your thinking. It will outgrow your old habits. Purpose will not let you live beneath your privileges. If you feel restless, stretched, or unsettled, it may not be because something is wrong. It may be because something is calling you to a higher place.

Purpose is not passive. It is persistent. You have to pursue it. Protect it. Prioritize it. Walk toward it even when you don't fully understand it.

I am living proof that purpose can be wrapped in pain—and still be purpose. Some of the most defining moments of my life were also the most confusing and hurtful. But now I see: nothing was wasted. Not one tear. Not one delay. Not one closed door. All of it was shaping me. All of it was preparing me. All of it was moving me—slowly, deliberately—toward who I was created to be. I now understand what it really means when it is said: It is your purpose in life to discover your purpose in life. And discovery is not a moment. It is a walk. A daily yes. A daily surrender. A daily decision to keep moving forward—even when the road is unclear. Purpose is not something you trip over. It is something you choose to walk into. On purpose. What if the steps you take today are the foundation of your future? How will you choose

to walk into your purpose tomorrow?

# Conclusion: Given Up for a Reason

For a long time, I believed my story began with abandonment. Now I know it began with an assignment. What once felt like rejection, I now recognize as redirection. What once felt like loss, I now see as placement. What once felt like being overlooked, I now understand was God quietly arranging my steps long before I ever knew I was being led. I was not forgotten. I was being positioned. It took me years to see this clearly. Years to understand that God is not reactive—He is strategic. He does not improvise with lives. He architects them. He does not waste pain. He weaves it. He does not abandon people. He assigns them. Others may have given me up. But God picked me up. And He did not do it impulsively. He did it intentionally. Looking back now, I can trace His hand through every chapter—through the adoption, the detours, the delays, the disappointments, the pit seasons, and the hidden years. Even when I couldn't see Him, He was shaping me. Even when I didn't understand Him, He was guiding me. Even when I tried to disqualify myself, He never changed His mind. Before I ever chose Him, He chose me. Before anyone celebrated me, He claimed me. Before anyone believed in me, He wrote me into His plan. My life is not proof that pain doesn't exist.

My life is proof that pain is not the end. Somewhere along the way, my story stopped being just mine. God began using it as a bridge for people who feel forgotten, overlooked, displaced, or discarded. People who wonder if where they started has permanently defined where they can go. I have watched eyes fill with tears when I say, "I was adopted." I have heard voices shake when people whisper, "So was I." I have seen hope return to faces that had quietly made peace with despair. That is when I understood: God never wastes a story. He redeems it. If you have walked through abandonment, you are not disqualified. If you have been given up, you are not forgotten. If your life has taken turns you never would have chosen, you are not lost. You are in process. And the process is not punishment. It is preparation. I do not know every detail of what God still has planned for my life. But I know this: I am no longer confused about why my story began the way it did. I was not given up by accident. I was given up on purpose. Because God had a purpose. And He is still fulfilling it.

# Reflection & Discussion Guide

Personal Reflection Questions

In what ways have you ever felt rejected, abandoned, or overlooked?

How has your past shaped how you see yourself today?

What part of your story have you struggled to accept?

Where do you see God's hand now that you didn't recognize before?

What would it look like to fully embrace your purpose?



What does *Given Up on Purpose* mean to you?

Which chapter impacted you the most and why?

How can pain become preparation?

What is the difference between being rejected by people and chosen by God?

How can we help others walk into purpose despite their past?

Journal Prompt

“If I truly believed nothing in my life was wasted,

I would . . .”

# Prayers & Declarations

A Prayer for the Reader

Father, I thank You that nothing in my life was accidental. Heal every wound, restore every broken place, and redeem every painful memory. I receive Your purpose, Your plan, and Your destiny for my life. I release the past and step into the future You designed for me. In Jesus' name, Amen.

Declarations

I am not a mistake. I am God's design.

My past does not disqualify me—it prepares me.

What was meant to break me, God is using to build me.

I walk in purpose on purpose.

Nothing in my life was wasted.

# Acknowledgments

First and foremost, I give all glory, honor, and praise to God. He is the Author and Finisher of my faith, the Redeemer of my story, and the One who took what could have broken me and used it to reveal His purpose. None of this exists without Him.

To my adoptive parents, Mildred and Milton Cooper—thank you for choosing me, loving me, raising me, and covering me. Your prayers, sacrifices, discipline, and unwavering commitment gave me a foundation that shaped the man, husband, father, and pastor I am today. I am forever grateful for the life you gave me—not just naturally but also spiritually.

In loving memory of my father—though

he is no longer with us, I honor his place in my

life and story. His legacy, influence, and the

lessons drawn from our relationship remain part

of the strength and perspective I carry today. I

acknowledge him with respect and remembrance.

To my birth mother, Linda Lewis—thank

you for giving me life. Our story has not been

without complexity, but I honor the fact that you

chose to carry me, chose not to abort me, and

gave me a chance to live. Because of that

decision, this book, this life, and this purpose

exist.

To my daughters, Amari and Ariyah—you

are two of my greatest gifts. You inspire me to

live intentionally, love deeply, and lead faithfully.

Everything I do, I do with you in mind. I pray that

my life, my faith, and my obedience to God will always point you to your own purpose.

To Pastor John Hannah—thank you for your prophetic voice in my life, for speaking with clarity and authority, for rebuking fear off of me, and for providing the confirmation I needed to walk boldly into this season. Thank you also for agreeing to write the foreword to this book. Your obedience and encouragement mean more to me than you know.

To my wife, Lady Chataira—thank you for standing with me through every season—seen and unseen. Your strength, love, prayers, and unwavering support have been a constant source of encouragement and stability in my life.

To my family, my spiritual leaders and mentors, and The Miracle Hub—thank you for your love, trust, and partnership in purpose.

To every friend, supporter, encourager, and challenger who pushed me forward—thank you. Some of you prayed for me. Some corrected me. Some opened doors. Some spoke life into hard seasons. All of you played a part. This journey carries your fingerprints.

And to every person who has ever felt rejected, abandoned, or overlooked—this book is proof that your story is not over, and your life is not an accident.

Nothing was wasted.

# About the Author

Aljenon Cooper is a pastor, leader, author, and visionary who serves as the Senior Pastor of The Miracle Hub (Miracle Church of God in Christ) in Los Angeles, California. He is also the Regional President of the International Youth Department Southwest Region for the Church of God in Christ.

Adopted at birth and raised by a praying, faith-filled woman, Pastor Cooper's life is a living testimony of God's redemptive power and divine intentionality. Through personal loss, rejection, leadership wounds, and seasons of deep questioning, God shaped him into a voice of hope, healing, and purpose for this generation.

He is passionate about helping people discover purpose, walk in wholeness, and live intentionally. His ministry centers on transformation, restoration, and empowering others to see that nothing in their life has been wasted.

*Given Up on Purpose* is his first book.

# Connect with Pastor Cooper

Thank you for reading *Given Up on Purpose*. My prayer is that this book encouraged you, strengthened your faith, and helped you see that your story still carries purpose.

I would love to stay connected with you and continue the journey together.

Website:

www.adlcministries.com

Social Media:

Instagram: @adlcministries

Facebook: www.facebook.com/ADLCMinistries

YouTube: ADLC Ministries

TikTok: @preach_coop

Ministry:

The Miracle Hub

Los Angeles, California

For speaking engagements, ministry invitations, and book-related inquiries, please visit the website or send a message through social media.

Stay encouraged. Stay in purpose. Your story is not over.

—Pastor Aljenon Cooper